Some days sne's tequila & other days, she's tea

Mermaid Poetry

BookLeaf Publishing

India | USA | UK

Presentation by *BookLeaf Publishing*

Web: www.bookleafpub.com

E-mail: info@bookleafpub.com

ISBN: 978-93-5744-381-4

First edition 2022

DEDICATION

To JJ, my half-orange and unwavering supporter.

PREFACE

This collection of poems explores my reawakening, falling in love, and our subsequent exploration of ethical non-monogamy.
It tells the story of discovery regarding the depth and breadth of love, our capacity for sharing sexual intimacy with more than one person, and the incredible joys that positive, conscious communication can bring. It is an ode to a relationship sustained through long-distance love, global pandemics, and personal challenge.

A fling before I leave...

First date
Butterflies
By the car
Waiting
#phwoar

Endless chat
Legs brushing
Paying the bill
She beats me to it
#sneaky

Walking back
Hand in pocket
Mine sneaks in
Don't freak out
#unexpected

Goodbye time
Her cheek
My lips
We kiss
#clumsybeautiful

Don't judge a book by its cover...

She used to think I was a hippy mum
Placenta-eating, chakra-honouring
Sweet but maybe dumb
But when I shaved my head
Kicked my husband out of the bed
Changed my glasses
Started signing up to classes
Stopped giving a fuck
What the people who truly suck
Thought about me
She could finally see
My colours true
Bursting through
She helped me feel alive again
Feel so young again
Learn how to love and trust again
Became my lover and my friend
Even when we thought this amazing thing
Would have to end

My confidence grew like new shoots on a fallen
tree
She helped me to be free

Unleashed my creativity
Realised I was so much more
Than what she knew before
A woman to adore
The crucial part
Of why our hearts
Align so well
Our core values match each other's
Integrity and wit and electricity between the
covers
Emboldened by her affection,
I grew
And flew
Born anew

From Princess to Queen

He called me his Princess,
which I liked at first,
feeling desired and cared for,
precious and young

But it became problematic,
in subtle ways,
a perceived imbalance,
in the scales of our relationship

I felt like a Princess, a child,
stuck in the ways of old,
going nowhere, standing still,
progressive no more.

You call me your Queen,
evoking images of Cleopatra,
strong and powerful in my own right,
independent and free

A more equitable pairing,
queens together, you and I,
building each other up,
and leading with our hearts

This Queendom makes my soul sing,
I want us to reign over our love,
side by side and hand in hand,
limbs and minds intertwined.

A collection of Haiku

The sea: gushing waves
Drowning me in their darkness
Your lips draw me in

*

Appears on the trees
Cherry blossom in the spring
Like kisses from you

*

Your first orgasm
Exploding like a burst pipe
Exquisite pain: gush!

*

Kissing you makes me
Warm and wet and oh so fine
I love your sweet lips

*

The leaves of my mind
Blow away when you touch me
Floating in the breeze

Whirling

You hula for me,
completely naked:
exposed

I start at the top, appreciating your beauty,
my gaze lingering on each part of you

Your eyes, a colour I can't describe,
grey-blue like an overcast sky, drawing me in

Your lips, soft and tender, fall slightly open
as you see me look at you

Your hair cascades over your shoulders,
making me want to run my hands through it and
brush it from your neck

Your slender neck, that I have kissed so many
times
but cannot get enough of

Your arms move as you keep the hoop from
falling,

stabilising and adjusting your balance

Those arms that have encircled me
as the hoop encircles your waist

Your long fingers and elegant wrists make slight
movements in the air,
reminding me of your touch over and inside of
me

Your perfect breasts stare me in the face, nipples
erect
at the thought of me watching you

My gaze moves downwards, away from your
face and down over your stomach,
echoing the path of kisses I make on my journey
from lips to lips

Your sensual hips move round and round,
hypnotising me with their rhythmic sway

I fantasise about holding onto those hips and
drawing you close,
my breasts against your back

The mound of your sex captivates me,
beckoning me towards it,

thinking of the warmth and familiarity that lies
inside

You turn and I can see your beautiful ass,
gentle thrusts as you hula around

Your legs are strong and powerful, I think of the
way they close around my head
when I am loving you with my tongue

Delicate ankles, adorned with your double
entendre tattoo,
connecting to your feet and the ground below

Watching you drives me insane

I want you
I crave you
I need you

Falling

"I think I'm in love",
said the bee to the flower,
slurping up nectar
from within her folds

Sunlight danced upon her wings
as she kissed her petals softly,
drank in her sweet scent,
and bathed in her perfume

But the flower did not respond,
for she knew that the bee
would soon move on
to another bloom

Leaving behind a trail of pollen
from her coated legs,
and the memory of her kisses,
warm upon her sepals

Missing kissing (and so much more)

In these times,
Where we can't touch,
Can't kiss,
Can't fuck,
Unless you're lucky enough
To be home
Locked down in one place
With a person
Whose face
Brings you joy
Makes you sing -
Only you are allowed
To do these things

But for the rest of us,
Alone in isolation
The best we can hope for
Is soft porn
And masturbation
A light titillation,
Maybe a video chat or two
Watching them
Watching you

Do you
'Cos what else is there to do?

Sure, there are chores
And projects galore
That I could be doing
Now I'm stuck indoors
But with the absence
Of the one I adore
My motivation lacks
I crave a firm touch
On my back
Begin to appreciate more
The massage therapist next door
The woman who strokes my skin
As I drift in and out
Of sleep,
Her touch relaxing my doubt

My arms prickle
From a lack of skin on skin
Thoughts of firm fingers
And warm kisses
Drawing me in
I dream of the curve
Of your body in mine
Arms in a tangle
And legs intertwined

And my mind yearns
For you
And the closeness of us
Bodies that fit
Like two moulded pieces
Of a perfect model kit
But I will wait
And make do
With the contact we have
Virtual and free
With your laugh
And your gaze
And thoughts of you and me

Long distance loving

I wanna pack a picnic
of all the foods we love
and take you to the forest
to watch the sky above

See the sun set in the distance
in the same fucking time zone
comfort you and cuddle you
so you know you're not alone

I wanna kiss you softly
and kiss you fierce and strong
we know we'll get to do this
but we cannot know how long

How long we have to wait
sometimes it seems so far
what I wouldn't give right now
to be with you where you are

Is she real?

It seems to me,
that she
could be
a figment
of my imagination.
Could my mind,
prone to machination,
have invented
her blue grey eyes
like soulful skies,
peach pink lips,
and sensual hips,
her laugh, from deep within
that draws me in,
skin so soft and tender,
one touch and she can render
me
helpless,
hopeless,
head-over-heels, lest
we part
and my heart
can't bear this duration,

the lack of sensation.
Sex over the phone
with her,
is still the best I've had,
but never
have I wanted something this bad.
My mind plays tricks
as tongue over teeth licks,
and memories kick
my consciousness.
She must be real,
surely I cannot have conjured
this way I feel,
so certain,
like never before,
knocking down doors
to get to her.
I would travel oceans
to turn up at her door
and hold her once more,
But I can't.
This current life,
logistic strife,
plans halted by a pandemic,
attempting to curtail
a connection endemic
to us,
as I have to trust

that we will survive this,
the thought of
just
one
kiss
is keeping me afloat,
despite the lack of boat,
no vessel to take me to you,
so what can I do?
Except fantasise
about those eyes
casting their gaze
of love and admiration
past nation after nation,
to stare upon my face,
video-calling software in place,
as we chase
our dream.
Sometimes the thought of you
seems too good to be true,
so I wonder,
is she real?
Or do I feel this way
for nought,
that thought
messes with my mind
when I feel I'm on borrowed time,
when I feel low

and the blow
of cancelled flights
and lonely nights
knocks me down.
But then I remember
her face,
her touch,
the way she sees through me
and straight into my soul,
the love I have for her,
and I concur -
she exists,
in more than just my dreams
and on my screens,
for she is in me,
heart and soul,
and that
will never grow old.

Our boy

A happy accident,
your involvement in this,
organically grown
and we haven't even kissed

But connected in mind
and in heart we are,
bodies virtually entwined,
even from afar

Your kindness and love
knows no limits,
support from you
and all it brings us

Is worth letting
ourselves be
this vulnerable
and this free

Imaginings

Your lips on my skin as he watches,
the thrill of being seen,
our consciences clean
as we move between
each other, as if in a dream,
and he touches himself while you touch me

He wants to taste our flavours,
your fingers plunge in,
my moans drown out the din,
sweet not saccharin
as he licks me off you, without sin
and relishes in my wetness

My tongue probes your cunt,
my mouth on your clit,
baby this is it
none of us want to quit,
I kiss him when you permit
and he tastes you from my lips

His cock is ready,
raring to go,
he feels down below,
gentle and slow
and then fast with the flow
as he brings himself to a satisfying finish

Rev(o/e)l(u/a)tion

A revolution is an insurrection -
An uprising against the oppressive feelings that
held me down,
Defined me by my roles,
Constrained me

This transformation is a liberation -
A rush of freedom bursting forth from within,
A selfish act,
In a good way

My development is a revelation -
A move forward on this previously static life
train,
Pushing me onwards,
Enabling growth

This new chapter is a rediscovery -
Opening me up to reveal my true self once
again,
As I was before,
Only different

Compersion

I watch as he fucks you,
bent over
facing me
while you can see
two screens,
showing my wet dreams,
your face
and your body,
a spectacular show
made better by knowing
that while his erection is growing,
you are thinking of me,
my face is what you see
that first time he thrusts into you
and you moan
down the phone
while I wait in our home
for my FOMO to go

I chase compersion
like it will make me a better person
and I know
I should go
and let you get on with the show,

but I stay too long
and for a moment, it feels wrong
until I remember our song
and I do trust in you,
I know your intentions are true
and it is me you desire,
me who lights the fire
in your soul as well as your loins

So I don't mind
if you spend a while
with a man and his dimpled smile,
his ever-growing cock,
that you seem to love to suck,
his massage bench and big strong hands.
I am glad
that you get
some company
while we
cannot be physical,
existing in this digital world
for a time.
Before we know it, we will find
we are back in each other's arms
and I am calm
once again

FOMO

I get mad at the world
for this situation we are in -
there is no sin
on your part,
it's just my fears
and irrational FOMO
bursting at the seams.

In my dreams,
I can rise above
the gut-punch feels
and be generous
in my affections
and my permissions,
so you can be generous
with yours.

The doors
this lifestyle opens for us
and the relief it brings,
are more than worth
the occasional angst
and I am grateful
for your observations

and how you
respect
my illogical reactions
with your quick actions
and the love you show me.

These moments
when jealousy rises within me,
are the times
when my fingers drift
towards switching profiles
and reading your messages,
but I will not torment myself today
reading into things
that just aren't there,
because I care
about you
and about honesty and trust
and checking up on each other
is just not us.

I am so sure
about you
and about us
and I believe
in everything we do,
but you
mean so much to me,

that sometimes to see
someone else doting on you
in ways I currently cannot do
makes my insides twitch
and perhaps
I ought to switch
off the screen
that's making me scream.
But, like the macabre,
I can't look away
so I stay
glued to my phone
feeling more alone
than I should,
because in reality
I know I am your priority
I just can't help that,
occasionally,
the love in my heart
needs some help,
to quieten the voices in my head

Valid

I'm sorry
when feelings of resentment
and jealousy
bubble up from within my core.
It's not fair on you
and they are my reaction to own,
but I'm thankful
for you
for listening
for letting me share
for holding space for my feelings and me,
no matter how irrational we are

Getting used to this

You treat me like a fucking treasure,
a precious gem you have discovered
and hold proudly aloft -
I am not used to this

You value my worth like I have never known,
listen to my voice when I talk and talk,
actively seek my opinion -
I am not used to this

You say I am a diamond,
not the lump of rock I once felt like,
now sparkly and new -
I am not used to this

You know I am a prize,
someone you are proud to know,
a joy to behold -
I am not used to this

Thank you,
I am believing it more every day -
I am not used to this,

but I am getting there

Ethical Slut

An ethical slut, I think I am,
as we explore this polyam,
relationshiply anarchistic life.
Monogamish,
I wish,
that more people
would open doors,
instead of shutting gates
and putting up
arbitrary boundaries
that tie them
to societal norms,
while we form
a fantastically explorative
life together,
be my wife and we can date together,
no hate for this weather,
no storms for us,
as we storm this bus.
Haters get off
and go home
to be alone,
while we reap the benefits
of good communication

and sexual exploration
Our bond strengthened
By bonds with another
Your lover is my lover
We share bodies and minds
Yet still find
That what we have
Is one of a kind

New friends

New friends, now more than acquaintances,
satisfied with a situation this
delicious, filled with carnal delights,
our sexual desires ignite
as we fight
the urge to jump you,
and instead, take it slow,
go with the flow,
until before you know
it, a quivering mess
of bodies rests,
satisfied, spent, fulfilled,
this throuple of will.
A cunting good time had by all,
as we fall:
for you, into you, onto you, with you.
It's true
that sex can be fun,
but this was next level!
So thank you,
for your touch, your trust,
your tongue and your lust,
for your generous loving,
next time we must

continue to explore, with skin on skin,
draw further in
to this exciting adventure,
perhaps venture
to other corners
of the kink world
and see what we find.
But until then,
use your mind
to recall the delights
and sights
of last night's
ecstasy.

Backlash

"Cover up"
you say,
as if masking
a woman's flesh
diminishes her
sexual value,
hides her desires,
renders her
no longer
a risk

But this,
I tell you,
is a
cover up -
how you want me
to cover my legs
and up
my game,
disguise my skin
as it makes you
uncomfortable

I will not

be party
to this societal
wave
crashing over
the heads of women
who have been taught
to stay small,
after all,
you want me
to cover up
as my flesh
offends your
prudish sensibilities

But your argument
is a double-faced
sword
plunging into
my naked depths -
does that
offend you?
The mention
of my nakedness,
like the day
I was born

Thirsty

Drink me up like a hot cup of tea, slurp me, the
first sip burning your tongue, scorching, tingling

Put me in your pipe and smoke it, toke it, inhale
me like your favourite scent, get high on my
fumes and never come down

Inject me like a drug, shoot me up, coursing
through your bloodstream like erythrocytes
laden with oxygen

Tattoo me on your body, mark my name on your
skin, painful and permanent, a lasting reminder
of me

Bathe in me, soak in my touch, like water
slightly too hot, uncomfortable and raw, 'till the
skin on your fingertips wrinkles, but yet you stay

Drive me, ride me, a motorcycle hot between
your strong thighs, rev me and feel my power
underneath you

Bleed me, when you are cut open, sticky and
wet, slow to clot, seeping away

Fall into me, disappear, a deep well, a black hole
in the night sky, time warping and the moon
waxing and waning

Walk over me like hot coals, burning your feet,
flames moving up and licking your body as I
consume you

Fuck the patriarchy

This poem
Is for the "too much"
Women
The sexually free
And want to be me
Women
The I love myself
And I'm
Not
Afraid
To say it
Women

This poem
Is for
The women
Who
Laugh loudly
And cry even louder
The women
Who show up
And grow up,
The women
Who tell their

Friends
"I love you"

This poem
Is for
The freedom fighters
And the librarians
The anarchists
And the introverts
The women
Who don't take shit
From no-one
The women
Who drive fast
And eat slowly
The women
Who savour life
Every
Last
Delicious
Fucking
Drop of it

This poem
Is for
The young women
Finding their place
In the world

For the
Old women
Who dye their hair
And ride motorcycles
Right over
Your expectations
Of how
They should behave

This poem
Is for the women
Who know
That you don't need
A uterus
To be a woman
The women
Who don't give time
To negative energy
And cut that shit
Out of their lives
The women
With anxiety
And the women
Who had to see a doctor
Twenty times
Before they were diagnosed

This poem

Is for the women
Who love to travel
The women
Who open doors
And climb
Over barriers
The women
Who are quiet
As a mouse
But when they speak
You know it was
Worth the wait

This poem
Is for the women
Who pole dance
The women who do ballet
And the women who do both
The women
Who love music
Or reading
So much
That they
Get lost in it
For hours

This poem
Is for

The women
Who were called demure
But
Can't
Take
It
No more
The women
Who want to smash shit up
The women
Who want to stand up
The women
Who want to live it up

This poem
Is for the women
Who speak up
The women
Who call out
Hypocrisy
And mediocrity
The women
Who say
"Can you repeat that?"
When verbally abused
Under the breath
Of someone
Who doesn't know their privilege

The women
Who show their braveness
And wear their hearts
On their sleeves

This poem
Is for the women
Who cry at adverts
The women
With
So much
Compassion
That they save ants
On the sidewalk
The women
Who protest
And take placards
To the streets
The women
Who don't miss a beat
And challenge
Sexism

This poem
Is for the women
Who practice
Self-care
By organising

Their calendar
And cooking healthy meals
And getting enough sleep
The women
Who drink to forget
And the women
Who stay sober
To remember
The women
Who take long baths
And longer walks
And the women
Who just want
A
Second
To
Themselves

This poem
Is for the women
With a high IQ
And a high EQ
The women
Whose empathy
Means they feel
Every
Crack
On

This
Precious
Earth
The women
Who remember birthdays
And book appointments

That aren't for them
Who take on
The emotional labour
Of an army

This poem
Is for the women
Who stay out dancing
Until three o'clock
The up all night women
Living their
Best life women
And giving
Zero fucks
The women
Who are shy
And the women
Who don't need
A drink
To get on that stage
And sing their

Bloody hearts out

This poem
Is for the women
Who don't think
That tampons
Are taboo
The women
Who celebrate
Their cycles
And worship
The changing of the moon
The women
Who generate stares
When they walk
Into a room
The women
You suggest to
'Smile'
But they'd rather frown
The women
Whose generosity
Knows no bounds

This poem
Is for the women
Who teach their children
Their genitals' proper names

The women
Who aren't afraid
When their toddler
Shouts "vulva!"
When they're trying to get changed
The women
Facing racism
Through no fault of their own
The women
Who work three jobs
To give their kids a home

This poem
Is for the rebel women
With, or without, a cause
The women
Who knock on doors
That society
Tried to close
To them
The women
Who smash
Glass ceilings
And explode
Tired patriarchal tropes
Of femininity
Like fireworks
On New Year's Eve

This poem
Is for the women
Of the resistance
For feminists
And Marxists
And the women
Who just
Don't give a shit

This poem
Is a whisper
And a shout
An anthem
For the lost
And the found

This poem
Is for me
And for you